COOK ONCE EAT TWICE

chicken • beef • slow cooker • and more

Publications International, Ltd.

Favorite Brand Name Recipes at www.fbnr.com

Favorite Brand Name Recipes is a trademark of Publications International, Ltd.

Photography on back cover and pages 4, 5, 19, 71, 79, 81, 87, 89, 115 and 117 by Maes Studio.
Photographer: Mike Maes
Photographer's Assistants: Jillian McDaniel and Benjamin Stern
Food Stylist: Dianne Hugh-Freeze
Assistant Food Stylist: Ingrid Askim

Pictured on the front cover *(left to right):* Italian-Style Pot Roast *(page 42)* and Tortilla Beef Casserole *(page 44)*.

Pictured on the back cover *(left to right):* Marinated Italian Sausage & Peppers *(page 78)* and Sausage & Pepper Pizza *(page 80)*.

ISBN-13: 978-1-4127-1673-4
ISBN-10: 1-4127-1673-X

Library of Congress Control Number: 2008935012

Manufactured in China.

8 7 6 5 4 3 2 1

Microwave Cooking: Microwave ovens vary in wattage. Use the cooking times as guidelines and check for doneness before adding more time.

TABLE OF CONTENTS

INTRODUCTION

DAY 1 IS COOK DAY. DAY 2 IS QUICK DAY.

Turn tonight's delicious dinner into tomorrow's feast! The Day 1 recipes in *Cook Once Eat Twice* are designed to yield extras that quickly come together in a delightful family meal on Day 2 with minimal effort.

THINK AHEAD.

Whether you're roasting a ham, slow cooking chicken thighs or grilling vegetables, it doesn't take any longer to make a little more. Then, instead of revisiting the same meal the next day, turn it into something new and different the whole family will love. Who could resist Sausage & Pepper Pizza, made with leftovers from yummy Marinated Grilled Sausages & Peppers? Or how about turning a beef lover's Balsamic-Glazed Sirloin & Spinach into hearty Steak & Potato Skillet on Day 2 in minutes?

BE FLEXIBLE.

Only you know your family's tastes and appetites. Most recipes in *Cook Once Eat Twice* are created to yield 4 servings each day. Check out both recipes before you go to the market to see if there are changes you need to make. You may want to adjust quantities if family members are light eaters or if they have particularly hearty appetites (any teenage boys at the table?).

DAY

Balsamic-Glazed Sirloin
& Spinach (page 114)

DAY 2

Skillet Steak
& Potatoes (page 116)

STORE THINGS PROPERLY.

Be sure to refrigerate leftovers promptly. Don't leave dishes on tables or countertops to cool. If you have a large amount of hot food left over, divide it into smaller portions so it will cool more quickly. Ideally, food should be refrigerated within two hours. (The danger zone for bacterial growth is between 40°F and 140°F. The important thing is to get food out of this temperature range as quickly as possible.)

Store food in leakproof, preferably clear, containers, so you can see the contents. If you won't be able to use ingredients the next night, transfer them to the freezer. Most prepared foods freeze well, provided they are wrapped airtight and your freezer is at 0°F. Exceptions are creamy sauces and foods with a high water content, such as celery, leafy greens and the like.

DON'T CALL THEM LEFTOVERS!

With a bit of advance planning and the inspiring recipes in *Cook Once Eat Twice* you can banish the dreaded question, "Are we having that again?" Now instead of leftovers, you'll have two delicious meals for the work of one.

DAY 1

Marinated Italian Sausage
& Peppers (page 78)

DAY 2

Sausage & Pepper
Pizza (page 80)

ROASTS & MORE

ROAST CHICKEN WITH PEPPERS

Makes 4 servings plus leftovers for **Chicken Tetrazzini with Peppers & Mushrooms**

3½ to 4 pounds bone-in chicken pieces
3 tablespoons olive oil, divided
1 tablespoon plus 1½ teaspoons chopped fresh rosemary *or* 1½ teaspoons dried rosemary
1 tablespoon fresh lemon juice
1¼ teaspoons salt, divided
¾ teaspoon black pepper, divided
5 bell peppers (assorted colors)
1 medium onion

1. Preheat oven to 375°F. Place chicken in shallow roasting pan.

2. Combine 2 tablespoons oil, rosemary and lemon juice in small bowl; brush over chicken. Sprinkle 1 teaspoon salt and ½ teaspoon black pepper over chicken. Roast 15 minutes.

3. Cut bell peppers lengthwise into ½-inch-thick strips. Cut onion into thin wedges. Toss vegetables with remaining 1 tablespoon oil, ¼ teaspoon salt and ¼ teaspoon pepper in large bowl. Arrange vegetables around chicken; roast about 40 minutes or until vegetables are tender and chicken is cooked through (165°F). Serve chicken with vegetables and pan juices.

4. Cut leftover chicken off bones into bite-size pieces. Reserve and refrigerate with leftover pepper strips for Chicken Tetrazzini with Peppers & Mushrooms.

CHICKEN TETRAZZINI WITH PEPPERS & MUSHROOMS

Makes 4 servings

> 8 ounces uncooked egg noodles
> 3 tablespoons butter
> ¼ cup all-purpose flour
> 1 can (about 14 ounces) chicken broth
> 1 cup whipping cream
> 2 tablespoons dry sherry
> 2 cans (6 ounces each) sliced mushrooms, drained
> Bell pepper strips from Roast Chicken with Peppers
> Chopped chicken from Roast Chicken with Peppers (about 2 cups)
> 1 teaspoon Italian seasoning
> ½ cup grated Parmesan cheese

1. Cook egg noodles according to package directions. Drain; cover and keep warm.

2. Meanwhile, melt butter in medium saucepan over medium heat. Add flour and whisk until smooth. Gradually add chicken broth, stirring constantly; bring to a boil over high heat. Remove from heat. Gradually stir in cream and sherry until well blended.

3. Combine mushrooms, peppers and noodles in large bowl; toss well. Add half of sauce; stir. Combine remaining sauce, chicken and Italian seasoning in medium bowl.

4. Spoon noodle mixture onto serving plates. Top with chicken mixture. Sprinkle with cheese.

ONION-WINE POT ROAST

Makes 4 servings plus leftovers for **Italian Beef Ragu**

 2 tablespoons olive oil, divided
 1 teaspoon salt, divided
 ½ teaspoon black pepper
 1 boneless beef chuck roast (about 3 pounds), trimmed
 2 pounds yellow onions, cut in half and thinly sliced
 2 tablespoons water
 2 cups red wine, such as cabernet sauvignon or merlot

1. Heat 1 tablespoon oil in Dutch oven over medium-high heat. Sprinkle ½ teaspoon salt and pepper over beef; place in Dutch oven. Cook until beef is well browned on both sides, about 6 minutes per side. Transfer beef to large plate.

2. Preheat oven to 300°F. Add remaining 1 tablespoon oil, onions and ½ teaspoon salt to Dutch oven; cook over medium-high heat 10 minutes, stirring frequently. Stir in water, scraping up any browned bits from bottom of pan. Reduce heat to medium; partially cover and cook 15 minutes, stirring occasionally or until onions are deep golden brown.

3. Stir in wine. Return beef to pan with any juices accumulated on plate. Cover and bake about 3 hours or until beef is fork-tender.

4. Remove beef from Dutch oven. Slice or cut into large pieces; keep warm. Skim fat from juices; serve beef with juices. Reserve and refrigerate leftover pot roast and onions plus about ½ cup juices for Italian Beef Ragu.

Serving Suggestion: Serve pot roast over hot cooked mashed potatoes or orzo pasta.

ITALIAN BEEF RAGU

Makes 4 servings

> 1 tablespoon olive oil
> Pot roast, onions and juices from Onion-Wine Pot Roast (about 2½ cups total)
> 2 cans (about 14 ounces) fire-roasted diced tomatoes
> 1 teaspoon dried oregano
> 1 teaspoon dried basil
> ⅛ teaspoon red pepper flakes or black pepper
> 8 ounces uncooked fettuccine

1. Heat oil in large saucepan over medium heat. Add pot roast, onions and juices. Cook and stir 3 minutes, breaking up any large pieces of meat. Add tomatoes, oregano, basil and pepper flakes. Simmer, uncovered, 10 minutes, stirring occasionally.

2. Meanwhile, cook fettuccine according to package directions; drain. Evenly divide fettuccine among 4 serving plates or bowls. Top with equal amounts of beef ragu.

[TIP]

It's always a good idea to make enough pot roast to have plenty left over. In addition to turning it into Italian Beef Ragu, the possibilities are endless. There are the obvious (but delicious!) hot or cold pot roast sandwiches. The leftover beef also works in tacos or quesadillas. For an easy and tasty casserole, just substitute pot roast for ground beef in almost any recipe, such as tamale casserole or baked ziti.

DAY 1

BAKED HAM WITH SWEET & SPICY GLAZE

*Makes 6 to 8 servings plus leftovers for **Pineapple Ham Fried Rice***

1 bone-in smoked half ham (about 6 pounds)
Sweet and Spicy Glaze (recipe follows)

1. Preheat oven to 325°F. Place ham, fat side up, on rack in roasting pan. Roast 3 hours.

2. Meanwhile, prepare Sweet and Spicy Glaze. Brush half of glaze over ham; bake 30 minutes or until meat thermometer registers 160°F. Brush with remaining glaze. Let stand 20 minutes before slicing. Reserve and refrigerate leftover ham for Pineapple Ham Fried Rice.

SWEET & SPICY GLAZE

Makes about 2 cups

$^3\!/_4$ cup packed brown sugar
$^1\!/_3$ cup cider vinegar
$^1\!/_4$ cup golden raisins
1 can (8$^3\!/_4$ ounces) sliced peaches in heavy syrup, drained, chopped and syrup reserved
1 tablespoon cornstarch
$^1\!/_4$ cup orange juice
1 can (8$^1\!/_4$ ounces) crushed pineapple in syrup, undrained
1 tablespoon grated orange peel
1 clove garlic, minced
$^1\!/_2$ teaspoon red pepper flakes
$^1\!/_2$ teaspoon grated fresh ginger

1. Combine brown sugar, vinegar, raisins and peach syrup in medium saucepan. Bring to a boil over high heat. Reduce heat to low; simmer 8 to 10 minutes.

2. Dissolve cornstarch in orange juice in small bowl; add to brown sugar mixture. Add remaining ingredients; mix well. Cook over medium heat, stirring constantly, until mixture boils and thickens.

DAY 2

PINEAPPLE HAM FRIED RICE

Makes 4 to 6 servings

Ham from Baked Ham with Sweet & Spicy Glaze
3 tablespoons vegetable oil, divided
2 tablespoons sliced almonds
1 small green bell pepper, cut into strips
2 green onions, coarsely chopped
4 cups cooked white rice, cooled
1 can (8 ounces) pineapple chunks packed in juice, undrained
2 tablespoons raisins
2 to 3 tablespoons soy sauce
1 tablespoon dark sesame oil

1. Cut leftover ham into bite-size pieces. You will need about 2 cups.

2. Heat wok over medium-high heat 1 minute. Drizzle 1 tablespoon vegetable oil into wok and heat 30 seconds. Add almonds; stir-fry until golden brown. Remove from wok.

3. Add remaining 2 tablespoons vegetable oil to wok and heat 30 seconds. Add ham, bell pepper and onions; stir-fry 2 minutes. Add rice, pineapple with juice and raisins; stir-fry until heated through.

4. Stir in soy sauce and sesame oil; stir-fry until well mixed. Transfer to serving bowl. Sprinkle with almonds just before serving.

[TIP]

Cook the rice on Day 1 while the ham is in the oven. Let it cool to room temperature, then transfer it to a food storage container. Refrigerate until needed on Day 2.

TERIYAKI PORK & MANGO SALSA

Makes 4 servings plus leftovers for **Thai Basil Pork Stir-Fry**

- 2 pounds pork tenderloin (2 or 3 tenderloins)
- 1 cup teriyaki sauce
- 2 large mangoes, peeled and cut into bite-size pieces
- ½ red onion, minced
- 1 or 2 jalapeño peppers,* minced
- 3 cloves garlic, minced
- Juice of 2 limes
- 1 bunch cilantro, finely chopped
- ¼ teaspoon salt

Jalapeño peppers can sting and irritate the skin, so wear rubber gloves when handling peppers and do not touch your eyes.

1. Place pork in large resealable food storage bag. Pour teriyaki sauce over pork; seal bag. Refrigerate 1 to 4 hours.

2. For salsa, place mango in medium bowl. Add onion, jalapeño and garlic. Gently stir in lime juice, cilantro and salt. Refrigerate until ready to serve.

3. Preheat oven to 375°F. Drain pork and place in roasting pan; discard marinade. Roast 25 to 35 minutes or until pork is barely pink in center (160°F). Slice and serve with mango salsa. Reserve and refrigerate leftover pork for Thai Basil Pork Stir-Fry.

DAY 2

THAI BASIL PORK STIR-FRY

Makes 4 to 6 servings

Pork from Teriyaki Pork & Mango Salsa
2 tablespoons canola oil
1 pound fresh broccoli florets
1 medium red bell pepper, cut into strips
1 to 2 tablespoons Thai green curry paste*
1¼ cups chicken broth
2 tablespoons chopped fresh basil
2 tablespoons finely chopped roasted peanuts
3 cups fresh mung bean sprouts

Thai green curry paste is available in the ethnic section of most supermarkets in cans or jars. Spiciness varies among brands, so check the label directions and adjust the amount used based on how spicy you want the dish.

1. Cut leftover pork into bite-size pieces. You will need about 1½ cups.

2. Heat oil in large nonstick skillet over high heat. Add broccoli; stir-fry 3 to 4 minutes or until broccoli begins to color. Add bell pepper; stir-fry 1 minute.

3. Add pork and curry paste; stir-fry 2 minutes. Add broth; cook and stir 2 to 3 minutes or until heated through.

4. Remove from heat; stir in basil. Sprinkle with peanuts and serve with bean sprouts.

[TIP]

Stir-fries are an excellent use for all kinds
of leftovers. Make use of small quantities of
leftover cooked vegetables by adding them to
the skillet or wok towards the end of cooking
time. Almost anything goes—green beans,
tomatoes, eggplant, onions. Just cut them into
bite-size pieces and add to the mix.

GREEK ROAST CHICKEN

Makes 4 servings plus leftovers for **Basque-Style Chicken & Pasta**

- 1 whole roasting chicken (4 to 5 pounds)
- 3 tablespoons olive oil, divided
- 2 tablespoons chopped fresh rosemary, plus 2 sprigs
- 2 cloves garlic, minced
- 1 small lemon
- 1¼ teaspoons salt, divided
- ½ teaspoon black pepper, divided
- 1 can (about 14 ounces) chicken broth, divided
- 2 large sweet potatoes, cut into thick wedges
- 1 medium red onion, cut into ¼-inch wedges
- 1 pound fresh asparagus spears, trimmed

1. Preheat oven to 425°F. Place chicken, breast side up, in shallow roasting pan. Combine 2 tablespoons oil, chopped rosemary and garlic in small bowl; brush over chicken.

2. Grate 1 teaspoon peel from lemon; set aside. Cut lemon into quarters; squeeze juice over chicken and place rinds and rosemary sprigs in chicken cavity. Sprinkle ¾ teaspoon salt and ¼ teaspoon pepper over chicken. Pour 1 cup broth into bottom of roasting pan; roast 30 minutes.

3. *Reduce oven temperature to 375°F.* Arrange sweet potatoes and onion wedges around chicken. Drizzle remaining broth and 1 tablespoon oil over vegetables; roast 15 minutes.

4. Arrange asparagus spears in roasting pan. Sprinkle remaining ½ teaspoon salt and ¼ teaspoon pepper over vegetables. Roast 10 minutes or until chicken is cooked through (165°F) and vegetables are tender. Transfer chicken to cutting board. Tent with foil; let stand 10 to 15 minutes.

5. Sprinkle reserved lemon peel over chicken. Serve with vegetables and pan juices. Cut leftover chicken off bones into bite-size pieces. Reserve and refrigerate for Basque-Style Chicken & Pasta.

BASQUE-STYLE CHICKEN & PASTA

Makes 4 servings

- 8 ounces thin spaghetti
- 2 tablespoons olive oil
- 1 medium onion, chopped
- 4 cloves garlic, minced
- 1 jalapeño pepper,* minced
- 1 jar (26 ounces) marinara or mushroom pasta sauce
- ¼ cup red wine or port wine (optional)
  Chicken from Greek Roast Chicken (about 2 cups chopped)
- ⅓ cup pimiento-stuffed olives, halved crosswise
- ¼ cup finely diced salami or prosciutto

Jalapeño peppers can sting and irritate the skin; wear rubber gloves when handling peppers and do not touch your eyes.

1. Cook spaghetti according to package directions. Drain; keep warm.

2. Meanwhile, heat oil in large saucepan over medium heat. Add onion, garlic and jalapeño; cook and stir 5 minutes. Add pasta sauce and wine, if desired; bring to a simmer, stirring frequently. Stir in chicken and olives; simmer 5 minutes.

3. Arrange pasta on 4 serving plates. Top with sauce; Sprinkle with salami.

Serving Suggestion: Serve with crusty whole grain rolls and a fruit salad.

[TIP]

This sauce freezes well. For a more pronounced olive flavor, prepare and freeze the sauce without the olives, and add them to the sauce when reheating.

DAY 1

ROAST TURKEY BREAST WITH SAUSAGE & APPLE STUFFING

Makes 6 servings plus leftovers for **Easy Cajun Turkey Stew**

8 ounces bulk pork sausage
1 medium apple, cored, peeled and finely chopped
1 shallot or small onion, finely chopped
1 stalk celery, finely chopped
¼ cup chopped hazelnuts
½ teaspoon rubbed sage, divided
½ teaspoon salt, divided
½ teaspoon black pepper, divided
1 tablespoon butter, softened
1 whole boneless turkey breast (4½ to 5 pounds), thawed if frozen
4 to 6 fresh sage leaves (optional)
1 cup chicken broth

1. Preheat oven to 325°F. Crumble pork sausage into large skillet. Add apple, shallot and celery; cook and stir until sausage is cooked through and apple and vegetables are tender. Drain fat. Stir in hazelnuts and ¼ teaspoon each sage, salt and pepper. Spoon stuffing into shallow roasting pan.

2. Combine butter and remaining ¼ teaspoon each sage, salt and pepper in small bowl. Spread over turkey breast. (Arrange sage leaves under skin, if desired.) Place rack on top of stuffing. Place turkey, skin side down, on rack. Pour broth into pan.

3. Roast 45 minutes. Remove turkey from oven; turn skin side up. Baste with broth. Return to oven; roast 1 hour or until cooked through (165°F). Let turkey rest 10 minutes before carving. Serve with stuffing. Reserve and refrigerate leftover turkey for Easy Cajun Turkey Stew.

EASY CAJUN TURKEY STEW

Makes 4 to 6 servings

2 tablespoons vegetable oil

1 red bell pepper, diced

1 stalk celery, sliced

1 can (about 14 ounces) diced tomatoes with roasted garlic and onions

1½ cups chicken broth

Turkey from Roast Turkey Breast with Sausage & Apple Stuffing

1 can (about 15 ounces) kidney beans, rinsed and drained

1 pouch (about 9 ounces) New Orleans-style chicken-flavored ready-to-serve rice mix

¼ teaspoon hot pepper sauce

¼ cup chopped green onions

1. Heat oil in Dutch oven over medium-high heat. Add bell pepper and celery; cook and stir 3 minutes. Add tomatoes and broth; bring to a boil.

2. Meanwhile, cut leftover turkey into bite-size pieces. You will need about 3 cups. Add turkey, beans, rice mix and pepper sauce to Dutch oven. Reduce heat to low. Cover; cook 7 minutes. Stir in green onions. Remove from heat. Cover; let stand 2 to 3 minutes to thicken.

Tip: If canned diced tomatoes with garlic and onions aren't available, substitute 1 can (about 14 ounces) diced tomatoes; add 1 teaspoon minced garlic and ¼ cup chopped onion to the bell pepper mixture.

THYME-SCENTED ROAST BRISKET DINNER

Makes 4 servings plus leftovers for **Quick Beef Bourguignonne**

- 1 beef brisket (4 to 5 pounds)
- 4 cloves garlic, minced
- 2 teaspoons dried thyme
- 1 teaspoon salt
- ½ teaspoon black pepper
- 2 large onions, thinly sliced
- 1 can (about 14 ounces) beef broth
- 2 pounds red potatoes, halved or quartered
- 1 pound baby carrots
- 2 tablespoons butter
- 2 tablespoons all-purpose flour

1. Preheat oven to 350°F.

2. Place brisket, fat side up, in large roasting pan; sprinkle with garlic, thyme, salt and pepper. Separate onion slices into rings; scatter over brisket. Pour broth over onions. Cover; roast 2 to 3 hours. Uncover; stir onions into drippings. Arrange potatoes and carrots around brisket. Cover; roast 45 minutes or until brisket and vegetables are fork-tender.

3. Transfer brisket to cutting board. Tent with foil; let stand 10 minutes. Transfer vegetables with slotted spoon to serving bowl; keep warm. Strain pan juices into measuring cup. Refrigerate 10 minutes or until fat rises to the surface. Spoon off fat.

4. Melt butter in medium saucepan over medium heat. Add flour; cook and stir 1 minute. Stir in juices; cook 3 to 4 minutes until sauce thickens, stirring constantly.

5. Slice brisket and serve with warm vegetables and sauce. Reserve and refrigerate leftover brisket, vegetables and sauce for Quick Beef Bourguignonne.

QUICK BEEF BOURGUIGNONNE

Makes 4 servings

> 3 slices bacon, diced
> 1 large onion, chopped
> 4 ounces sliced mushrooms
> 3 cloves garlic, minced
> 1 teaspoon dried thyme
> 1/4 teaspoon black pepper
> 2 tablespoons all-purpose flour
> 1 can (about 14 ounces) beef broth
> 1/2 cup burgundy or port wine
> Beef brisket from Thyme-Scented Roast Brisket Dinner
> Sauce from Thyme-Scented Roast Brisket Dinner (about 1 cup)
> Vegetables from Thyme-Scented Roast Brisket Dinner (about 3 cups)
> Chopped fresh parsley

1. Cook and stir bacon in large skillet over medium heat 5 minutes or until crisp. Transfer bacon to paper towel with slotted spoon; set aside.

2. Add onion to drippings in skillet; cook and stir 5 minutes. Add mushrooms, garlic, thyme and pepper; cook and stir 5 minutes. Sprinkle flour over vegetables; cook and stir 1 minute. Add broth and wine; bring to a boil over high heat, scraping browned bits off bottom of pan. Reduce heat; simmer, uncovered, 5 minutes or until slightly thickened, stirring occasionally.

3. Meanwhile, cut leftover brisket into bite-size pieces. You will need about 2 1/2 cups. Add brisket to stew; simmer 5 minutes. Stir leftover sauce and vegetables into stew; heat through. Ladle into shallow bowls; top with reserved bacon and parsley.

START WITH A SLOW COOKER

DAY 1

HAM WITH FRUITED BOURBON SAUCE

Makes 6 to 8 servings plus leftovers for **Ham & Cheddar Frittata**

> 1 bone-in ham, butt portion (about 6 pounds)
> ¾ cup packed dark brown sugar
> ½ cup raisins
> ½ cup apple juice
> 1 teaspoon ground cinnamon
> ¼ teaspoon red pepper flakes
> ⅓ cup dried cherries
> ¼ cup cornstarch
> ¼ cup bourbon, rum or apple juice

1. Coat 5-quart slow cooker with nonstick cooking spray. Add ham, cut side up. Combine brown sugar, raisins, apple juice, cinnamon and pepper flakes in small bowl; stir well. Pour evenly over ham. Cover; cook on LOW 9 to 10 hours or on HIGH 4½ to 5 hours. Add cherries 30 minutes before end of cooking time.

2. Transfer ham to cutting board. Let stand 15 minutes before slicing.

3. Pour cooking liquid into large measuring cup; let stand 5 minutes. Skim and discard excess fat. Return cooking liquid to slow cooker.

4. *Turn slow cooker to HIGH.* Whisk cornstarch and bourbon in small bowl until cornstarch is dissolved. Stir into cooking liquid. Cover; cook 15 to 20 minutes or until thickened. Serve sauce over sliced ham.

5. Reserve and refrigerate leftover ham for Ham & Cheddar Frittata.

DAY 2

HAM & CHEDDAR FRITTATA
Makes 4 servings

Ham from Ham with Fruited Bourbon Sauce
3 eggs
3 egg whites
½ teaspoon salt
½ teaspoon black pepper
1½ cups (4 ounces) frozen broccoli florets, thawed
⅓ cup roasted red bell pepper strips
1 tablespoon butter
½ cup (2 ounces) shredded sharp Cheddar
   cheese

1. Preheat broiler. Cut leftover ham into bite-size cubes. You will need about 1½ cups.

2. Beat eggs, egg whites, salt and black pepper in large bowl until blended. Stir in broccoli, ham and pepper strips.

3. Melt butter over medium heat in large ovenproof skillet with sloping side. Pour egg mixture into skillet; cover. Cook 5 to 6 minutes or until eggs are set around edge. (Center will be wet.)

4. Uncover; sprinkle cheese over frittata. Transfer skillet to broiler; broil 5 inches from heat 2 minutes or until eggs are set in center and cheese is melted. Let stand 5 minutes; cut into 4 wedges.

BARBECUED PULLED PORK

Makes 4 servings plus leftovers for **Pork Tacos with Roasted Green Onions**

> 1 boneless pork shoulder or butt roast (about 4 pounds)
> 1 teaspoon salt
> 1 teaspoon ground cumin
> 1 teaspoon paprika
> 1 teaspoon black pepper
> ½ teaspoon ground red pepper
> 1 medium onion, thinly sliced
> 1 medium green bell pepper, cut into strips
> 1 bottle (18 ounces) barbecue sauce
> ½ cup packed light brown sugar
> Sandwich rolls or hot cooked rice

1. Trim excess fat from pork. Combine salt, cumin, paprika, black pepper and red pepper in small bowl; rub over roast.

2. Place onion and bell pepper in 5-quart slow cooker; top with pork. Combine barbecue sauce and brown sugar in medium bowl; pour over pork. Cover; cook on LOW 8 to 10 hours.

3. Transfer roast to cutting board. Trim and discard remaining fat from roast. Pull pork into coarse shreds using 2 forks. Serve pork with sauce on sandwich rolls or over rice.

4. Reserve and refrigerate leftover pork mixture for Pork Tacos with Roasted Green Onions.

DAY 2

PORK TACOS WITH ROASTED GREEN ONIONS

Makes about 4 servings

- 8 green onions, trimmed
- 2 teaspoons olive oil
  Salt
- 8 soft corn tortillas
- 2 cups pork from Barbecued Pulled Pork, reheated

1. Preheat oven to 425°F. Place green onions on baking sheet and drizzle with oil; toss gently to coat. Arrange in single layer and bake 10 minutes. Season with salt.

2. Heat tortillas over burner or grill about 15 seconds per side or until lightly charred.

3. Place about ¼ cup pork mixture and a roasted green onion on half of each tortilla. Fold tortilla over filling.

[TIP]

Fresh pork shoulder roast is an economical and delicious cut of meat, though definitely on the fatty side. Roasts from the shoulder are also referred to as pork butt roast, pork blade roast, Boston butt or pork picnic. (The term "butt" comes from an old-fashioned name for barrels that pork was shipped in long ago. It does not refer to the rear of the animal.) With long, slow cooking, pork shoulder is tender and flavorful. In addition to sandwiches and tacos, pulled pork is perfect for stir-fries and casseroles.

ITALIAN-STYLE POT ROAST

Makes about 4 servings plus leftovers for
Tortilla Beef Casserole

2 teaspoons minced garlic
1 teaspoon salt
1 teaspoon dried basil
1 teaspoon dried oregano
¼ teaspoon red pepper flakes
1 boneless beef bottom round rump or chuck shoulder roast (about 2½ to 3 pounds)
1 large onion, quartered and thinly sliced
1½ cups tomato-basil or marinara pasta sauce
2 cans (about 15 ounces each) cannellini or Great Northern beans, rinsed and drained
¼ cup shredded fresh basil or chopped Italian parsley

1. Combine garlic, salt, dried basil, oregano and pepper flakes in small bowl; rub over roast.

2. Place half of onion slices in slow cooker. Cut roast in half. Place one half of roast over onion slices; top with remaining onion slices and other half of roast. Pour pasta sauce over roast. Cover; cook on LOW 8 to 9 hours or until roast is fork-tender.

3. Remove roast to cutting board; tent with foil. Let liquid in slow cooker stand 5 minutes to allow fat to rise. Skim off fat.

4. *Turn slow cooker to HIGH.* Stir beans into liquid. Cover; cook 15 to 30 minutes or until beans are hot. Slice roast and serve topped with bean mixture and fresh basil.

5. Cut leftover pot roast into bite-size pieces. Reserve and refrigerate for Tortilla Beef Casserole.

TORTILLA BEEF CASSEROLE

Makes 4 servings

Pot roast from Italian-Style Pot Roast (about 2 cups)
6 (6-inch) corn tortillas, cut into 1-inch pieces
1 jar (16 ounces) salsa
1½ cups corn
1 can (about 15 ounces) black or pinto beans, rinsed and drained
1 cup (4 ounces) shredded Mexican cheese blend

1. Preheat oven to 350°F. Lightly spray 11×7-inch baking dish or 2-quart casserole with nonstick cooking spray.

2. Combine beef, tortillas, salsa, corn and beans in large bowl; mix well. Transfer to prepared casserole.

3. Bake 20 minutes or until heated through. Sprinkle with cheese; bake 5 minutes or until cheese is melted.

[TIP]

Even a small amount of leftover meat can easily be turned into a casserole by combining it with starchy ingredients, such as beans or tortillas. Cooked potatoes or green vegetables could also be added to this recipe. Use your imagination and choose your family's favorites.

THAI-STYLE CHICKEN

Makes 4 servings plus leftovers for **Udon Noodles with Chicken & Spinach**

- 1 teaspoon ground ginger
- ½ teaspoon salt
- ¼ teaspoon ground red pepper
- 3½ pounds bone-in chicken pieces, skin removed
- 1 medium onion, chopped
- 3 cloves garlic, minced
- ⅓ cup canned coconut milk
- ¼ cup peanut butter
- 2 tablespoons soy sauce
- 1 tablespoon cornstarch
- 2 tablespoons water
- 3 cups hot cooked couscous or yellow rice
- ¼ cup chopped cilantro
  Lime wedges (optional)

1. Combine ginger, salt and red pepper in small bowl; sprinkle over meaty sides of chicken. Place onion and garlic in slow cooker; top with chicken. Whisk together coconut milk, peanut butter and soy sauce in medium bowl; pour over chicken. Cover; cook on LOW 6 to 7 hours or on HIGH 3 to 4 hours or until chicken is cooked through.

2. Transfer chicken to serving bowl with slotted spoon; cover with foil to keep warm. *Turn slow cooker to HIGH.* Combine cornstarch and water in small bowl until smooth. Stir into slow cooker. Cover; cook 15 minutes or until sauce is slightly thickened. Spoon sauce over chicken. Serve chicken over couscous; top with cilantro. Garnish with lime wedges.

3. Reserve and refrigerate leftover chicken for Udon Noodles with Chicken & Spinach.

UDON NOODLES WITH CHICKEN & SPINACH

Makes 4 servings

Chicken from Thai-Style Chicken
1 tablespoon vegetable oil
2 to 3 teaspoons grated fresh ginger
2 cloves garlic, minced
1 cup chicken broth
6 cups (6 ounces) coarsely chopped baby spinach
2 green onions, chopped
1 package (8 ounces) udon noodles, cooked and drained
1 tablespoon soy sauce

1. Remove leftover chicken from bones and cut into bite-size pieces. You will need about 2 cups.

2. Heat oil in large skillet. Add ginger and garlic; cook over low heat 20 seconds or until garlic begins to color. Add broth; bring to a simmer.

3. Stir in spinach and green onions. Cook 2 to 3 minutes or until spinach wilts. Stir chicken and noodles into spinach mixture. Season with soy sauce. Serve immediately.

SEARED PORK ROAST WITH CURRANT CHERRY SALSA

Makes 4 servings plus leftovers for **Cuban Pork Sandwiches**

1½ teaspoons chili powder
¾ teaspoon salt
½ teaspoon garlic powder
½ teaspoon paprika
¼ teaspoon ground allspice
   Nonstick cooking spray
1 boneless pork loin roast (about 3 pounds)
½ cup water
1 bag (16 ounces) frozen pitted dark cherries, thawed, drained and halved
¼ cup currants or dark raisins
1 teaspoon grated orange peel
1 teaspoon balsamic vinegar
⅛ to ¼ teaspoon red pepper flakes

1. Combine chili powder, salt, garlic powder, paprika and allspice in small bowl. Press spice mixture evenly onto roast.

2. Coat large skillet with cooking spray; heat over medium-high heat. Brown roast on all sides. Place in slow cooker.

3. Pour water into skillet, scraping up browned bits. Add to slow cooker. Cover; cook on LOW 6 to 8 hours or until pork is cooked through.

4. Remove roast from slow cooker. Tent with foil; keep warm. Strain juices from slow cooker; discard solids. Pour juices into small saucepan; keep warm over low heat.

5. *Turn slow cooker to HIGH.* For salsa, add cherries, currants, orange peel, vinegar and pepper flakes to slow cooker. Cover; cook 30 minutes.

6. Slice pork and serve with juices and salsa. Reserve and refrigerate leftover pork for Cuban Pork Sandwiches.

CUBAN PORK SANDWICHES

Makes 4 servings

1 tablespoon yellow mustard
4 crusty bread rolls, split in half
   Pork from Seared Pork Roast with Currant
      Cherry Salsa
4 slices Swiss cheese
4 thin ham slices
2 small dill pickles, thinly sliced lengthwise

1. Spread mustard on both sides of rolls. Arrange pork slices on roll bottoms. Top each with Swiss cheese slice, ham slice and pickle slices. Cover with top of roll.

2. Coat large skillet with nonstick cooking spray; heat over medium heat. Working in batches, arrange sandwiches in skillet. Cover with foil and top with dinner plate to press down sandwiches. (If necessary, weight with 2 to 3 cans to compress sandwiches lightly.) Heat until cheese is slightly melted, about 8 minutes. (Or use a tabletop grill or panini press to compress and heat sandwiches.) Serve immediately.

[TIP]

Leftover pork is quite versatile. Try creating a simple southwestern stir-fry by adding it to sautéed bell peppers and onions. Quesadillas are another easy, foolproof way to utilize pork. Layer pork and shredded cheese between two tortillas. Heat in a skillet until the cheese melts and serve with salsa for a quick and delicious lunch or dinner.

PROVENÇAL LEMON & OLIVE CHICKEN

Makes 4 servings plus leftovers for **Tuscan Chicken with White Beans**

- 2 cups chopped onions
- 8 skinless chicken thighs (about 2½ pounds)
- 1 lemon, thinly sliced and seeds removed
- 1 cup pitted green olives
- 1 tablespoon olive brine from jar or white vinegar
- 2 teaspoons herbes de Provence
- 1 bay leaf
- ½ teaspoon salt
- ⅛ teaspoon black pepper
- 1 cup chicken broth
- ½ cup minced fresh parsley

1. Place onions in slow cooker. Arrange chicken thighs over onions. Place lemon slice on each thigh. Add olives, brine, herbes de Provence, bay leaf, salt and pepper. Slowly pour in broth.

2. Cover; cook on LOW 5 to 6 hours or on HIGH 3 to 3½ hours or until chicken is tender. Remove and discard bay leaf. Stir in parsley.

3. Cut leftover chicken off bones into bite-size pieces. Reserve and refrigerate for Tuscan Chicken with White Beans.

[TIP]

It's best to use skinless chicken when cooking it in a slow cooker without browning first, or the color will be pale and the texture rubbery. To skin chicken easily, grasp the skin with a paper towel and pull it away. Be sure to clean the area thoroughly and wash your hands after handling raw chicken for food safety reasons.

TUSCAN CHICKEN WITH WHITE BEANS

Makes 4 servings

> 1 large bulb fennel (about ¾ pound)
> 1 teaspoon olive oil
>   Chicken from Provençal Lemon & Olive
>   Chicken (about 2 cups)
> 1 teaspoon dried rosemary
> ½ teaspoon black pepper
> 1 can (about 14 ounces) stewed tomatoes,
>   undrained
> 1 can (about 14 ounces) chicken broth
> 1 can (about 15 ounces) cannellini beans, rinsed
>   and drained
>   Hot pepper sauce (optional)

1. Cut off and reserve ¼ cup chopped feathery fennel tops. Chop bulb into ½-inch pieces. Heat oil in large saucepan over medium heat. Add chopped fennel bulb; cook 5 minutes, stirring occasionally.

2. Add chicken to saucepan; sprinkle with rosemary and pepper. Add tomatoes with juice and broth; bring to a boil. Cover; simmer 10 minutes. Stir in beans; simmer, uncovered, 10 to 15 minutes or until sauce thickens. Season with hot pepper sauce, if desired. Ladle into bowls; top with reserved fennel tops.

[TIP]

Canned beans in the cupboard are one of
a cook's best friends. They can easily turn
leftovers into a hearty stew or casserole and
also provide good nutrition with healthy
helpings of fiber and protein.

TURKEY BREAST WITH SWEET CRANBERRY–SOY SAUCE

Makes 6 servings plus leftovers for **Couscous Turkey Salad**

> 1 bone-in turkey breast (6 to 7 pounds),*
>   thawed if frozen
> 1 can (16 ounces) whole berry cranberry sauce
> 1 packet (1 ounce) dry onion soup mix
>   Grated peel and juice of 1 medium orange
> 3 tablespoons soy sauce
> 2 to 3 tablespoons cornstarch
> 1 to 1½ tablespoons sugar
> 1 to 1½ teaspoons cider vinegar
>   Salt and black pepper

You may substitute 2 (3½-pound) bone-in turkey breast halves, if desired.

1. Coat 6- or 7-quart slow cooker with nonstick cooking spray. Place turkey in bottom, meat side up. Reserve 2 tablespoons cranberry sauce; set aside in refrigerator for Couscous Turkey Salad. Combine remaining cranberry sauce, soup mix, orange peel and orange juice in small bowl. Pour over turkey. Cover; cook on HIGH 3½ hours or until cooked through (165°F).

2. Scrape cranberry mixture into cooking liquid. Transfer turkey to cutting board. Let stand 15 minutes before slicing.

3. Combine soy sauce and cornstarch in small bowl until smooth. Stir into cooking liquid with sugar and vinegar. Season with salt and pepper. Cover; cook on HIGH 15 minutes or until thickened slightly. Serve sauce over sliced turkey.

4. Reserve and refrigerate leftover turkey for Couscous Turkey Salad.

DAY 2

COUSCOUS TURKEY SALAD

Makes 4 servings

    1 cup plus 2 tablespoons chicken broth
    ¼ teaspoon salt
    ¾ cup uncooked pearl or Israeli couscous*
        Turkey from Turkey Breast with Sweet
          Cranberry-Soy Sauce
    1 cup shredded carrots (2 medium carrots)
    1 stalk celery, trimmed and finely chopped
    1 green onion, trimmed and chopped
    2 tablespoons toasted pine nuts

Dressing

    2 tablespoons reserved cranberry sauce from
        Turkey Breast with Sweet Cranberry-Soy
        Sauce
    2 tablespoons vegetable oil
    1 tablespoon plus 1 teaspoon balsamic vinegar
    ½ teaspoon curry powder
    ¼ teaspoon salt
    ¼ teaspoon pepper

*Pearl or Israeli couscous is the size of small pearls. If you can't find it, substitute regular couscous.

1. For salad, combine broth and salt in small saucepan. Bring to a boil. Stir in couscous. Cover and reduce heat to low. Simmer 3 to 5 minutes or until liquid is absorbed and couscous is tender. Transfer couscous to medium bowl. Refrigerate until cold.

2. Meanwhile, cut leftover turkey into bite-size pieces. You will need about 1⅓ cups. Combine turkey, carrots, celery, green onion and pine nuts in large bowl. Stir in couscous.

3. For dressing, stir together cranberry sauce, oil, vinegar, curry powder, salt and pepper. Pour over salad; toss well.

GRILLING PLUS

RED SNAPPER WITH AVOCADO-PAPAYA SALSA

Makes 4 servings plus leftovers for **Fish Tacos with Yogurt Sauce**

- 1 teaspoon ground coriander
- 1 teaspoon paprika
- ¾ teaspoon salt
- ⅛ to ¼ teaspoon ground red pepper
- ½ cup diced ripe avocado
- ½ cup diced ripe papaya
- 2 tablespoons chopped fresh cilantro
- 1 tablespoon lime juice
- 2 to 2½ pounds red snapper or halibut fish fillets
- 1 tablespoon olive oil
- 4 lime wedges

1. Oil grill grid. Prepare grill for direct cooking. Combine coriander, paprika, salt and red pepper in small bowl or cup; mix well.

2. For salsa, combine avocado, papaya, cilantro, lime juice and ¼ teaspoon spice mixture in medium bowl; set aside.

3. Brush fish with oil; sprinkle with remaining spice mixture. Grill fish, covered, over medium-high heat 10 minutes or until fish begins to flake when tested with fork, turning once. Serve with salsa and lime wedges.

4. Reserve and refrigerate leftover fish for Fish Tacos with Yogurt Sauce.

DAY 2

FISH TACOS WITH YOGURT SAUCE

Makes 4 servings

Sauce

- ½ cup plain yogurt
- ¼ cup chopped cilantro
- 3 tablespoons sour cream
- Juice of 1 lime
- 1 tablespoon mayonnaise
- ½ teaspoon ground cumin
- ¼ teaspoon ground red pepper
- Salt and black pepper

Tacos

- Red snapper from Grilled Red Snapper with Avocado-Papaya Salsa
- 8 corn or flour tortillas
- 3 cups shredded cabbage or prepared coleslaw mixture
- 2 medium tomatoes, chopped

1. For sauce, mix yogurt, cilantro, sour cream, lime juice, mayonnaise, cumin and red pepper in small bowl. Season with salt and black pepper to taste.

2. Flake fish or break into large pieces. You will need about 1½ cups. Place tortillas on burner or on grill over medium heat. Cook 10 seconds per side or until beginning to brown lightly.

3. Fill tortillas with fish, cabbage, tomatoes and sauce.

GINGER-LIME CHICKEN THIGHS

Makes 4 servings plus leftovers for **Fiesta Chicken Sandwich**

- ⅓ cup vegetable oil
- 3 tablespoons lime juice
- 3 tablespoons honey
- 2 teaspoons grated fresh ginger *or* 1 teaspoon ground ginger
- ¼ to ½ teaspoon red pepper flakes
- 1½ pounds boneless skinless chicken thighs

1. Combine oil, lime juice, honey, ginger and pepper flakes in small bowl. Place chicken in large resealable food storage bag. Add ½ cup marinade. Seal bag; turn to coat. Marinate in refrigerator 30 to 60 minutes, turning occasionally. Reserve and refrigerate remaining marinade.

2. Prepare grill for direct cooking.

3. Remove chicken from marinade; discard marinade. Grill chicken over medium-high heat 12 minutes or until cooked through (165°F), turning once. Brush with reserved marinade during last 5 minutes of cooking.

4. Reserve and refrigerate leftover chicken for Fiesta Chicken Sandwich.

[TIP]

Grilling is a great way to create extras for the next night's dinner. It's easy and economical to cook some extra meat or veggies while the fire is hot. Next time you light the grill, give yourself some delicious Day 2 options.

FIESTA CHICKEN SANDWICH

Makes 2 servings

Chicken from Ginger-Lime Chicken Thighs
1 tablespoon olive oil, plus extra for brushing
½ onion, sliced
½ medium red bell pepper, sliced
½ cup guacamole
2 (8-inch) pizza crusts
6 slices (1 ounce each) pepper jack cheese

1. Slice leftover chicken. You will need about 1 cup.

2. Heat 1 tablespoon oil in large nonstick skillet over medium-high heat. Add onion and bell pepper; cook and stir 3 to 4 minutes or until crisp-tender. Remove vegetables with slotted spoon.

3. Layer guacamole, chicken, vegetables and cheese evenly on one pizza crust; top with remaining pizza crust. Brush sandwich lightly with oil.

4. Heat same skillet over medium heat. Add sandwich; cook 4 to 5 minutes per side or until cheese melts and sandwich is golden brown. Cut into wedges to serve.

ITALIAN VEGETARIAN GRILL

*Makes 4 servings plus leftovers for **Gemelli &
Summer Vegetables***

4 large bell peppers, cored and quartered
4 medium zucchini, cut horizontally into ½-inch
    thick slices
1 pound asparagus (about 20 spears)
2 large red onions, cut into ½-inch-thick rounds
½ cup olive oil
2 teaspoons salt, divided
1 teaspoon Italian seasoning
1 teaspoon black pepper, divided
1 cup uncooked polenta
4 cups water
4 ounces goat cheese, crumbled

1. Arrange bell peppers, zucchini and asparagus in single layer on
1 or 2 baking sheets. To hold onion together securely, pierce slices
horizontally with metal skewers. Add to baking sheet. Combine oil,
1 teaspoon salt, Italian seasoning and ½ teaspoon black pepper in
small bowl. Brush mixture generously over vegetables, turning to coat
all sides.

2. Prepare grill for direct cooking. Meanwhile, bring water to a boil with
remaining 1 teaspoon salt in large saucepan. Whisk in polenta gradually.
Reduce heat to medium. Cook, stirring constantly, until polenta thickens
and begins to pull away from side of pan. Stir in remaining ½ teaspoon
black pepper. Keep warm.

3. Grill vegetables over medium-high heat, covered, 10 to 15 minutes,
turning once. Remove when tender. Place bell peppers in large bowl.
Cover; let stand 5 minutes. When cool enough to handle, peel off
charred skin. Cut all vegetables into bite-size pieces.

4. Serve polenta topped with vegetables and sprinkled with goat
cheese. Reserve and refrigerate leftover vegetables for Gemelli &
Summer Vegetables.

GEMELLI & SUMMER VEGETABLES

Makes 4 servings

8 ounces uncooked gemelli or rotini pasta
2 tablespoons pine nuts
1 clove garlic
1 cup packed fresh basil leaves
3 tablespoons olive oil
¼ cup grated Parmesan cheese
¼ teaspoon salt
¼ teaspoon black pepper
   Grilled vegetables from Italian Vegetarian Grill (about 2 cups)
1 cup grape or cherry tomatoes

1. Cook pasta according to package directions. Drain; keep warm.

2. Meanwhile, prepare pesto. Process pine nuts and garlic in food processor until coarsely chopped. Add basil; process until finely chopped. While processor is running, add oil. Stir in cheese, salt and pepper.

3. Place grilled vegetables in large bowl. Add pasta and tomatoes. Stir in pesto; toss to coat. Serve immediately.

CARNE ASADA

Makes 4 servings plus leftovers for **Speedy Beef Fajitas**

6 (6- to 8-ounce) thin skirt steaks
1½ teaspoons salt
¼ cup vegetable oil
2 jalapeño peppers,* minced
3 tablespoons fresh lime juice
4 cloves garlic, minced
1 cup (4 ounces) shredded Chihuahua cheese or Mexican cheese blend
¼ cup chopped cilantro

Jalapeño peppers can sting and irritate the skin. Wear rubber gloves when handling peppers and do not touch your eyes.

1. Season steaks with salt. Place in resealable food storage bag. Combine oil, jalapeños, lime juice and garlic in small bowl; pour over steaks. Seal bag; turn to coat. Refrigerate at least 2 hours or up to 24 hours.

2. Prepare grill for direct cooking. Drain steaks; reserve marinade. Grill steaks, covered, over medium-high heat 5 minutes. Brush with half of marinade. Turn; brush with remaining marinade. Grill 3 to 4 minutes for medium-rare (145°F) or until desired doneness.

3. Combine cheese and cilantro in small bowl; sprinkle over 4 steaks. Grill until cheese melts, about 1 minute.

4. Reserve and refrigerate 2 steaks without cheese for Speedy Beef Fajitas.

SPEEDY BEEF FAJITAS

Makes 4 servings

> Steaks from Carne Asada
> 8 flour tortillas
> 1 tablespoon vegetable oil
> 1 small red onion, sliced
> 1 *each* small red and green bell pepper, cut into thin strips
> 1 teaspoon ground cumin or chili powder
> ¾ cup chunky salsa
> 1 cup (4 ounces) shredded Chihuahua cheese or Mexican cheese blend
> ¼ cup chopped cilantro

1. Preheat oven to 350°F. Cut leftover steaks crosswise into strips. Stack and wrap tortillas in foil. Warm in oven 8 to 10 minutes or until heated through.

2. Meanwhile, heat oil in large nonstick skillet over medium-high heat. Add onion, peppers and cumin; cook and stir 4 to 5 minutes or until crisp-tender.

3. Add steak strips; cook and stir until steak is hot. Add salsa; cook and stir 1 minute. Serve mixture in warm flour tortillas topped with cheese and cilantro.

[TIP]

Fajitas are traditionally made from skirt steak cooked with onions and peppers as in this recipe, but feel free to invent your own variations. Serve an array of garnishes to make things even more interesting. Guacamole, sour cream, refried beans and additional salsa would all be delicious.

MARINATED ITALIAN SAUSAGE & PEPPERS

Makes 4 servings plus leftovers for **Sausage & Pepper Pizza**

$\frac{1}{2}$ cup olive oil
$\frac{1}{4}$ cup red wine vinegar
2 tablespoons chopped fresh parsley
1 tablespoon dried oregano
2 cloves garlic, crushed
1 teaspoon salt
1 teaspoon black pepper
6 hot or sweet Italian sausage links
2 large onions, cut into rings
2 large bell peppers, cut into quarters
Horseradish-Mustard Spread (recipe follows)

1. Combine oil, vinegar, parsley, oregano, garlic, salt and black pepper in small bowl. Place sausages, onions and bell peppers in large resealable food storage bag; pour oil mixture into bag. Seal bag; turn to coat. Marinate in refrigerator 1 to 2 hours.

2. Prepare Horseradish-Mustard Spread; set aside. Prepare grill for direct cooking.

3. Drain sausages, onions and bell peppers; reserve marinade. Grill sausages over medium heat, covered, 5 minutes. Turn sausages and place onions and bell peppers on grid. Brush sausages and vegetables with reserved marinade. Discard remaining marinade. Grill, covered, 5 minutes or until sausages are cooked through (160°F) and vegetables are crisp-tender. Serve with Horseradish-Mustard Spread.

4. Reserve and refrigerate leftover sausages, onion and bell pepper for Sausage & Pepper Pizza.

Horseradish-Mustard Spread: Combine 3 tablespoons mayonnaise, 1 tablespoon chopped fresh parsley, 1 tablespoon prepared horseradish, 1 tablespoon Dijon mustard, 2 teaspoons garlic powder and 1 teaspoon black pepper in medium bowl. Mix well.

DAY 2

SAUSAGE & PEPPER PIZZA

Makes 4 servings

⅟₂ cup tomato sauce

1 small garlic clove, minced

⅟₂ teaspoon dried basil

⅟₂ teaspoon dried oregano

⅛ teaspoon red pepper flakes (optional)

Grilled sausages from Marinated Italian Sausage & Peppers

Grilled onion and pepper from Marinated Italian Sausage & Peppers

1 (12-inch) prepared pizza crust

1⅟₂ cups (6 ounces) shredded fontina or pizza cheese blend

⅟₂ cup grated Parmesan cheese

1. Preheat oven to 450°F. Combine tomato sauce, garlic, basil, oregano and red pepper flakes, if desired, in small bowl. Cut sausages in half lengthwise, then crosswise into ⅟₂-inch slices. Cut onion and bell pepper into 1-inch pieces.

2. Place pizza crust on pizza pan or baking sheet. Spread tomato sauce mixture over crust, leaving 1 inch border. Sprinkle fontina cheese over tomato sauce; top with sausage, onion and bell pepper. Sprinkle with Parmesan cheese.

3. Bake about 12 minutes or until crust is crisp and cheese is melted.

CHICKEN ADOBO
Makes 4 servings plus leftovers for **Tacos Dorados**

$\frac{1}{2}$ cup chopped onion

$\frac{1}{3}$ cup lime juice

6 cloves garlic, coarsely chopped

1 teaspoon ground cumin

1 teaspoon dried oregano

$\frac{1}{2}$ teaspoon dried thyme

$\frac{1}{4}$ teaspoon ground red pepper

1$\frac{1}{2}$ to 2 pounds boneless skinless chicken breasts

3 tablespoons chopped fresh cilantro (optional)

1. Combine onion, lime juice and garlic in food processor. Process until onion is finely minced. Transfer to resealable food storage bag. Add cumin, oregano, thyme and red pepper; knead bag until blended. Place chicken in bag; press out air and seal. Turn to coat chicken with marinade. Refrigerate 30 minutes or up to 4 hours.

2. Spray grid with nonstick cooking spray. Prepare grill for direct cooking. Remove chicken from marinade; discard marinade. Grill chicken over medium heat 5 to 7 minutes per side or until chicken is no longer pink in center. Transfer to clean serving platter; garnish with cilantro.

3. Cut leftover chicken into bite-size pieces. Reserve and refrigerate for Tacos Dorados.

TACOS DORADOS

Makes 4 servings

2 tablespoons vegetable oil
½ cup chopped onion
1 can (28 ounces) whole tomatoes, cut up and juice reserved
2 teaspoons chili powder
1 teaspoon ground cumin
½ teaspoon salt
½ teaspoon garlic powder
½ teaspoon dried oregano
¼ teaspoon ground coriander
Chicken from Chicken Adobo (about 1½ to 2 cups)
3 cups (12 ounces) shredded queso blanco*
8 flour tortillas
¼ cup chopped fresh cilantro
Salsa

Queso blanco is white Mexican cheese. It is available in most large supermarkets and in Mexican markets. Mexican cheese blend may be substituted.

1. Heat oil in large skillet over medium-high heat. Add onion; cook and stir until translucent. Add tomatoes with juice, chili powder, cumin, salt, garlic powder, oregano and coriander. Cook 15 minutes, stirring frequently, until thickened. Add chicken; mix well.

2. Preheat oven to 450°F. Divide chicken mixture between tortillas; roll up tightly. Place, seam side down, in 13×9-inch baking dish. Bake 15 minutes or until tortillas are crisp and brown. Sprinkle with queso blanco; bake 5 minutes or until cheese is melted. Sprinkle with cilantro; serve with salsa.

DAY 1

GREEK LAMB WITH TZATZIKI SAUCE

Makes 4 to 6 servings plus leftovers for
Mediterranean Lamb Stew *or* **Lamb Pitas**

2½ to 3 pounds boneless leg of lamb
8 garlic cloves, divided
¼ cup Dijon mustard
2 tablespoons minced fresh rosemary
2 teaspoons salt
2 teaspoons black pepper
¼ cup plus 2 teaspoons olive oil, divided
1 small seedless cucumber
1 tablespoon chopped fresh mint
1 teaspoon lemon juice
2 cups Greek or other thick plain yogurt

1. Untie and unroll lamb leg to lie flat; trim fat.

2. For marinade, mince 4 garlic cloves. Combine garlic, mustard, rosemary, salt and pepper in small bowl. Whisk in ¼ cup oil. Spread evenly over both sides of lamb. Place lamb in large resealable food storage bag. Seal; refrigerate at least 2 hours or overnight, turning several times.

3. Meanwhile, prepare Tzatziki Sauce. Mince remaining 4 garlic cloves and mash to a paste; place in medium bowl. Peel and grate cucumber; squeeze to remove excess moisture. Add cucumber to bowl. Mix in mint, remaining 2 teaspoons oil and lemon juice. Add yogurt; stir until well combined. Refrigerate until ready to serve.

4. Prepare grill for direct cooking. Cook lamb over medium-high heat 35 to 40 minutes or to desired doneness. (Remove from grill at 140°F for medium. Temperature will rise 5°F while resting.) Transfer lamb to cutting board. Tent with foil; let rest 5 to 10 minutes.

5. Slice and serve with Tzatziki Sauce. Reserve and refrigerate leftover lamb and sauce for Mediterranean Lamb Stew or Lamb Pitas.

MEDITERRANEAN LAMB STEW
Makes 4 servings

- 1 tablespoon olive oil
- 1 medium red onion, chopped
- Lamb from Greek Lamb with Tzatziki Sauce, cut into bite-size pieces (about 2 cups)
- 1 can (about 14 ounces) diced tomatoes with green chiles
- 1 can (about 15 ounces) cannellini beans, rinsed and drained
- ¼ cup chopped fresh cilantro
- Pita bread
- Tzatziki Sauce from Greek Lamb with Tzatziki Sauce (optional)

1. Heat oil in large skillet over medium heat. Add onion; cook and stir 5 minutes. Add lamb and tomatoes. Cook, stirring occasionally, 5 minutes.

2. Stir in cannellini beans; cook until heated through. Sprinkle with cilantro. Serve with pita bread and Tzatziki Sauce, if desired.

LAMB PITAS
Makes 4 servings

- 1 cup Tzatziki Sauce from Greek Lamb with Tzatziki Sauce
- 4 pita bread rounds, cut in half
- Lamb from Greek Lamb with Tzatziki Sauce, cut into bite-size pieces (about 2 cups)
- 1½ cups diced tomatoes
- 1 cup shredded lettuce

Spoon 1 or 2 teaspoons Tzatziki Sauce into each pita half and fill with lamb, tomatoes and lettuce. Serve with remaining sauce.

SESAME-GARLIC FLANK STEAK

Makes 4 servings plus leftovers for **Seared Asian Steak Salad**

- 2 pounds beef flank steak
- 2 tablespoons soy sauce
- 2 tablespoons hoisin sauce
- 1 tablespoon dark sesame oil
- 2 cloves garlic, minced
    Stir-Fried Spinach with Garlic (recipe follows)

1. Score steak lightly with sharp knife in diamond pattern on both sides; place in large resealable food storage bag. Combine soy sauce, hoisin sauce, sesame oil and garlic in small bowl; pour over steak. Seal bag; turn to coat. Marinate in refrigerator at least 2 hours or up to 24 hours, turning once.

2. Prepare grill for direct cooking.

3. Drain steak; reserve marinade. Grill over medium heat, covered, 13 to 18 minutes for medium-rare (145°F) or to desired doneness, turning and brushing with marinade halfway through cooking time. Discard remaining marinade.

4. Transfer steak to cutting board; carve across the grain into thin slices. Serve with Stir-Fried Spinach with Garlic.

5. Reserve and refrigerate leftover steak for Seared Asian Steak Salad.

Stir-Fried Spinach with Garlic: Heat 1 tablespoon olive oil in large skillet over medium-high heat. Add 2 minced garlic cloves. Stir-fry 1 minute. Add 2 bunches (about 1 pound) torn, stemmed spinach and 1 tablespoon soy sauce. Stir-fry about 2 minutes or until spinach is wilted. Sprinkle with 2 teaspoons toasted sesame seeds before serving.

DAY 2

SEARED ASIAN STEAK SALAD

Makes 4 servings

> 1 bag (5 ounces) spring greens
> ½ cup thinly sliced red onion
> 1 cup thinly sliced red bell pepper
> 1 cup snow peas
> 1 medium carrot, cut into matchstick-size pieces
>   (½ cup)
> Steak from Sesame-Garlic Flank Steak
> 3 tablespoons hoisin sauce
> 1 teaspoon grated orange peel
> 2 tablespoons orange juice
> 2 tablespoons cider vinegar
> 2 tablespoons packed dark brown sugar
> 2 teaspoons dark sesame oil
> 1 teaspoon grated fresh ginger
> ⅛ teaspoon dried red pepper flakes

1. Arrange equal amounts of greens, onion, bell pepper, snow peas and carrots on four dinner plates. Top with sliced steak.

2. Whisk together hoisin sauce, orange peel, juice, vinegar, sugar, sesame oil, ginger and pepper flakes in small bowl. Drizzle over salads.

[TIP]

Topped with leftover steak or chicken, a main course salad served with crusty bread can be a filling meal even for hearty eaters. To make it even more filling, add sliced hard-cooked egg, avocado or croutons.

DELICIOUS DUOS

DAY 1

SPAGHETTI & MEATBALLS

Makes 4 servings plus leftovers for **Spicy Meatball Sandwiches**

> Nonstick cooking spray
> 1¼ pounds ground beef
> ½ pound hot turkey Italian sausage, casing removed
> 1 egg
> ¼ cup plain dry bread crumbs
> 1 teaspoon dried oregano
> 8 ounces uncooked multigrain or whole wheat spaghetti
> 1 jar (26 ounces) tomato-basil pasta sauce
> 2 tablespoons grated Parmesan cheese
> 3 tablespoons chopped fresh basil

1. Preheat oven to 450°F. Coat baking sheet with cooking spray. Combine beef, sausage, egg, bread crumbs and oregano in medium bowl; mix well. Shape meat mixture into 24 meatballs.

2. Place meatballs on prepared baking sheet; coat meatballs with cooking spray. Bake 12 minutes, turning meatballs once. Meanwhile, cook spaghetti according to package directions. Drain; keep warm.

3. Pour pasta sauce into large skillet; add meatballs. Cook and stir over medium heat about 9 minutes until sauce is hot and meatballs are cooked through. Serve spaghetti topped with half of meatballs and sauce; sprinkle with cheese and basil.

4. Reserve and refrigerate leftover meatballs and sauce for Spicy Meatball Sandwiches.

SPICY MEATBALL SANDWICHES

Makes 4 servings

12 meatballs with sauce from Spaghetti & Meatballs
   Additional pasta sauce as needed
½ cup chopped green bell pepper
⅓ cup sliced black olives
2 teaspoons Italian seasoning
¼ teaspoon ground red pepper
4 slices mozzarella cheese, halved lengthwise
4 hoagie buns
3 tablespoons shredded Parmesan cheese

1. Combine meatballs, sauce, bell pepper, olives, Italian seasoning and red pepper in large saucepan. (If mixture appears too dry, add additional pasta sauce.) Cook and stir over medium-high heat until bubbly and heated through.

2. Place two pieces of cheese on each bun. Spoon meatball mixture onto buns. Sprinkle with Parmesan cheese.

[TIP]

When freezing leftovers for later use, you need to remove as much oxygen as possible to prevent freezer burn and keep flavor intact. Choose a container that is as close to the volume of food as possible to eliminate air pockets. If freezing in a food storage bag with a zip top, close the bag almost all the way, insert a straw and suck out as much remaining air as possible before sealing the bag.

LEMON-ROSEMARY ROASTED CHICKEN

Makes 4 servings plus leftovers for **Cobb Salad**

1 (6- to 7-pound) chicken
1 teaspoon olive oil, divided
1 teaspoon salt, divided
¼ teaspoon black pepper
2 lemons
2½ teaspoons dried rosemary *or* 2 (4-inch) sprigs fresh rosemary, leaves chopped, divided
2 teaspoons butter, softened
1 cup chicken broth
½ teaspoon ground sage

1. Preheat oven to 450°F. Rub chicken with ½ teaspoon oil. Season with ½ teaspoon salt and pepper.

2. Pierce 1 lemon in several places with knife tip; place in chicken cavity. Blend 2 teaspoons rosemary and butter in small bowl. Carefully slide fingers under skin on breast to loosen. Gently smooth butter mixture under skin. Tie legs together with kitchen twine, if desired.

3. Place chicken on rack in roasting pan. Roast 45 minutes, then tent breast with foil. Roast 30 minutes or until chicken is cooked through (165°F), basting with pan drippings occasionally.

4. Transfer chicken to cutting board; let rest 10 minutes. Pour pan drippings into measuring cup; skim off fat. Squeeze juice from second lemon and add to drippings.

5. Return drippings to roasting pan; add any drippings from chicken. Add remaining ½ teaspoon salt, ½ teaspoon rosemary, broth and sage. Simmer over medium-high heat 2 minutes, scraping up browned bits from bottom of pan. Carve chicken; serve with sauce.

6. Cut leftover chicken off bones and dice. Reserve and refrigerate for Cobb Salad.

COBB SALAD

Makes 4 servings

Creamy Blue Cheese Dressing (recipe follows)
1 package (10 ounces) torn mixed salad greens
   or 8 cups torn romaine lettuce
Chicken from Lemon-Rosemary Roasted
   Chicken (about 1½ cups)
1 tomato, seeded and chopped
2 hard-cooked eggs, cut into bite-size pieces
4 slices bacon, crisp-cooked and crumbled
1 ripe avocado, diced
1 large carrot, shredded
1 ounce blue cheese, crumbled

1. Prepare Creamy Blue Cheese Dressing.

2. Place lettuce in serving bowl. Arrange chicken, tomato, eggs, bacon, avocado, carrot and cheese on top of lettuce. Serve with dressing.

CREAMY BLUE CHEESE DRESSING

Makes about ⅔ cup

½ cup mayonnaise
2 tablespoons crumbled blue cheese
1 tablespoon white wine vinegar
½ teaspoon dried dill weed
1 clove garlic, minced
1 teaspoon lemon juice

Mix all ingredients in small bowl; refrigerate until ready to use. Stir before serving.

SESAME PORK WITH THAI CUCUMBER SALAD

Makes 4 servings plus leftovers for **Better-Than-Take-Out Fried Rice**

> 3 pounds pork tenderloin (3 or 4 tenderloins)
> 1/4 cup soy sauce
> 4 cloves garlic, minced
>   Thai Cucumber Salad (recipe follows)
> 3 tablespoons honey
> 2 tablespoons brown sugar
> 1 teaspoon minced fresh ginger
> 1 to 2 tablespoons toasted sesame seeds

1. Place pork in large resealable food storage bag. Combine soy sauce and garlic in small cup; pour over pork. Seal bag; turn to coat. Marinate in refrigerator up to 2 hours. Meanwhile, prepare Thai Cucumber Salad and refrigerate.

2. Preheat oven to 400°F. Drain pork; reserve 1 tablespoon marinade. Combine honey, brown sugar, ginger and reserved marinade in small bowl. Place pork in shallow foil-lined roasting pan. Brush with half of honey mixture.

3. Roast 10 minutes. Turn pork over; brush with remaining honey mixture. Sprinkle with sesame seeds. Roast 10 to 15 minutes or until internal temperature is 155°F.

4. Transfer pork to cutting board. Tent with foil; let stand 5 minutes. (Temperature of pork will rise to 160°F.) Slice and serve with Thai Cucumber Salad. Reserve and refrigerate leftover pork for Better-Than-Take-Out Fried Rice.

Thai Cucumber Salad: Thinly slice 1 seedless cucumber and 1/2 red onion; combine in medium bowl. Combine 1/4 cup rice vinegar, 2 tablespoons lime juice and 1 teaspoon sugar in small bowl; stir into cucumber mixture. Cover; refrigerate 30 minutes. Stir in 2 tablespoons chopped fresh cilantro and 2 tablespoons chopped peanuts before serving. Makes 4 servings.

BETTER-THAN-TAKE-OUT FRIED RICE

Makes 4 servings

Pork tenderloin from Sesame Pork with
Thai Cucumber Salad
1 medium red bell pepper
3 tablespoons soy sauce
1 tablespoon rice vinegar
⅛ teaspoon red pepper flakes
1 tablespoon vegetable oil
6 green onions, cut into 1-inch pieces
1 tablespoon grated fresh ginger
1½ teaspoons minced garlic
2 cups shredded coleslaw mix
1 package (8½ ounces) cooked brown rice

1. Cut pork into bite-size pieces. You should have 1½ to 2 cups.

2. Cut bell pepper into bite-size pieces or, if desired, cut into decorative shapes with small cookie cutters.

3. Combine soy sauce, vinegar and red pepper flakes in small bowl; mix well.

4. Heat oil in large nonstick skillet or wok over medium-high heat. Add pork, bell pepper, green onions, ginger and garlic; stir-fry 1 minute. Stir in coleslaw mix and rice. Stir soy sauce mixture and add to skillet. Cook and stir 2 minutes or until heated through.

PICADILLO TACOS

Makes 4 servings plus leftovers for **Taco-Topped Potatoes** *or* **Taco Salad Supreme**

2 pounds ground beef
1 cup chopped green bell pepper
1 teaspoon ground cumin
1½ teaspoons chili powder
¼ teaspoon ground cinnamon
1 cup chunky salsa
8 (6- to 7-inch) corn tortillas, warmed
1 cup shredded lettuce
¾ cup (3 ounces) shredded Cheddar cheese
1 large tomato, chopped

1. Combine ground beef, bell pepper, cumin, chili powder and cinnamon in large nonstick skillet. Cook over medium heat 6 to 8 minutes, stirring to break up meat. Drain fat. Add salsa; reduce heat and simmer 5 minutes, stirring occasionally, or until beef is cooked through.

2. Fill tortillas with beef mixture, lettuce, cheese and tomato.

3. Reserve and refrigerate leftover beef mixture for Taco-Topped Potatoes or Taco Salad Supreme.

TACO-TOPPED POTATOES

Makes 4 servings

4 red or Yukon gold potatoes
Beef mixture from Picadillo Tacos
(about 1½ cups)
2 cups shredded lettuce
1 cup diced tomatoes
½ cup (2 ounces) shredded sharp Cheddar
cheese
½ cup sour cream

1. Poke potatoes with fork. Microwave on HIGH 6 to 7 minutes or until fork-tender. Meanwhile, cook and stir beef mixture over medium heat in medium saucepan until heated through.

2. Split potatoes almost in half; fluff with fork. Fill with beef mixture and top with lettuce, tomatoes, cheese and sour cream.

TACO SALAD SUPREME

Makes 4 servings

6 cups packed torn romaine lettuce
1 large tomato, chopped
Beef mixture from Picadillo Tacos
(about 1½ cups)
1 cup (4 ounces) shredded Mexican cheese
blend or taco cheese, divided
1 ripe avocado, diced
¼ cup sour cream

Arrange lettuce and tomato on 4 serving plates. Heat beef mixture in microwave or small saucepan until warm. Spoon over salad. Top with cheese, avocado and sour cream.

SPICY BARBECUED MEAT LOAF

*Makes 4 servings plus leftovers for **Easy Patty Melts***

1 to 2 slices rye bread, torn into pieces
1 large onion, cut into chunks
3 cloves garlic, peeled
1 tablespoon butter
1 pound ground beef chuck
1 pound bulk pork sausage
2 eggs
3/4 cup hickory-flavored barbecue sauce, divided
3/4 teaspoon salt
1/4 teaspoon black pepper

1. Preheat oven to 375°F. Line shallow roasting pan with foil.

2. Place bread in food processor; pulse until crumbs form. Transfer 3/4 cup bread crumbs to large bowl. (Any remaining crumbs may be frozen up to 3 months.) Add onion and garlic to food processor; process until finely chopped.

3. Melt butter in large skillet over medium heat. Add onion and garlic; cook 6 minutes or until softened, stirring occasionally. Let cool 5 minutes.

4. Add beef, sausage, eggs, 1/4 cup barbecue sauce, salt and pepper to reserved bread crumbs. Add onion mixture; mix well. Transfer meat mixture to prepared pan; shape into 9×6-inch oval.

5. Bake 30 minutes. Spread remaining 1/2 cup barbecue sauce over meat loaf. Bake 30 minutes more or until internal temperature reaches 160°F. Let stand 5 minutes before slicing.

6. Reserve and refrigerate leftover meat loaf for Easy Patty Melts.

EASY PATTY MELTS

Makes 4 servings

2 to 3 tablespoons butter, divided
1 large onion, thinly sliced
8 slices rye bread
8 slices Cheddar or mozzarella cheese
Meat loaf from Spicy Barbecued Meat Loaf

1. Heat 1 tablespoon butter in large skillet over medium-high heat. Add onion slices; cover and cook 5 minutes or until onion is transparent. Uncover; cook 8 to 10 minutes, stirring frequently, until onions are golden brown and very tender.

2. Top 4 bread slices with cheese slices; spoon onions evenly over cheese. Arrange slices of meat loaf over onions. Top with another cheese slice and remaining bread.

3. Melt 1 tablespoon butter in large skillet over medium heat. Add 2 sandwiches; cook 6 to 8 minutes per side or until golden brown and cheese is melted, turning every 2 minutes. Repeat with remaining sandwiches, adding butter to skillet as needed to prevent sticking.

[TIP]

When freezing leftovers for later use, be sure to
label them clearly with the date and contents.
Items like meat loaf or casseroles can be frozen
for at least one or two months if they are well
wrapped and if your freezer is 0°F or colder.

BALSAMIC–GLAZED SIRLOIN & SPINACH

Makes 4 servings plus leftovers for **Skillet Steak & Potatoes**

¼ cup plus 2 tablespoons olive oil, divided
2 Vidalia or other sweet onions, thinly sliced
2 tablespoons plus ½ teaspoon balsamic vinegar, divided
2 teaspoons salt, divided
2 pounds top sirloin steak
2 tablespoons coarsely ground black pepper
4 baking potatoes
1 bag (10 ounces) spinach, chopped

1. Heat 2 tablespoons oil in large skillet over medium-high heat. Add onions; cook 10 minutes or until softened, stirring occasionally. Sprinkle with 1 tablespoon balsamic vinegar and ½ teaspoon salt. Cook 10 minutes or until beginning to brown. Remove and keep warm.

2. Meanwhile, press 2 teaspoons pepper onto both sides of steak and rub with ½ teaspoon balsamic. Sprinkle with ½ teaspoon salt.

3. Poke potatoes with fork. Microwave on HIGH 8 minutes or until they yield to gentle pressure. Keep warm.

4. Heat 1 tablespoon oil in each of 2 large heavy skillets. (Skillet from onions may be used.) Add steaks and cook 5 minutes. Turn and cook 3 to 5 minutes for medium-rare (145°F) or to desired doneness. Transfer to serving platter and keep warm.

5. Add remaining 2 tablespoons oil to skillet; add spinach. Cover skillet until spinach wilts. Stir in remaining 2 tablespoons balsamic. Cook and stir 1 minute.

6. Cut steak into thin slices. Arrange over spinach and onions and serve with potatoes. Reserve and refrigerate leftover steak and 2 potatoes for Skillet Steak & Potatoes.

SKILLET STEAK & POTATOES

Makes 4 servings

Steak from Balsamic-Glazed Sirloin & Spinach
2 tablespoons olive oil
1 large onion, chopped
2 potatoes from Balsamic-Glazed Sirloin & Spinach, cut into bite-size pieces
1 teaspoon salt
½ teaspoon black pepper
½ teaspoon paprika
¼ teaspoon red pepper flakes
1 cup corn
1 cup halved grape tomatoes
¼ cup chopped parsley (optional)

1. Cut steak into bite-size pieces. You should have 1½ to 2 cups.

2. Heat oil in large heavy skillet over medium-high heat. Add onion; cook and stir 8 minutes or until beginning to brown. Add garlic; cook and stir 1 minute.

3. Add potatoes; stir to combine. Cook 4 minutes without stirring. Sprinkle with salt, black pepper, paprika and red pepper flakes. Stir, scraping up any browned bits from bottom of skillet.

4. Add corn, tomatoes and steak. Cook and stir until heated through. Garnish with parsley.

BUTTERMILK OVEN–FRIED CHICKEN

Makes 4 servings plus leftovers for **Sun-Dried Tomato Wraps with Fried Chicken**

2 cups buttermilk
1 tablespoon plus 1 teaspoon garlic powder, divided
2 teaspoons salt
2 teaspoons dried thyme, divided
1 teaspoon dried sage
1 teaspoon paprika
½ teaspoon black pepper
3½ to 4 pounds bone-in chicken pieces, skin removed
Nonstick cooking spray
2 cups panko bread crumbs*
¼ cup all-purpose flour

Panko bread crumbs are light, crispy, Japanese-style bread crumbs. They can be found in the Asian aisle of most supermarkets. Unseasoned dry bread crumbs may be substituted.

1. Whisk buttermilk, 1 tablespoon garlic powder, salt, 1 teaspoon thyme, sage, paprika and pepper in large bowl until well blended. Add chicken; turn to coat. Cover and refrigerate at least 5 hours or overnight.

2. Preheat oven to 400°F. Line 2 baking sheets with foil; spray with cooking spray. Combine bread crumbs, flour, remaining 1 teaspoon garlic powder and 1 teaspoon thyme in large shallow bowl. Remove chicken from buttermilk mixture, allowing excess to drip off. Coat chicken pieces one at a time with crumb mixture. Shake off excess crumbs. Place on prepared baking sheets; let stand 10 minutes.

3. Spray tops of chicken pieces with cooking spray. Bake about 50 minutes or until chicken is golden brown and cooked through (165°F), turning once and spraying with additional cooking spray halfway through baking time. Reserve and refrigerate leftover chicken for Sun-Dried Tomato Wraps with Fried Chicken.

SUN-DRIED TOMATO WRAPS WITH FRIED CHICKEN

Makes 4 servings

Chicken from Buttermilk Oven-Fried Chicken
½ cup ranch salad dressing
4 large sun-dried tomato flour tortillas, warmed
3 cups shredded lettuce
4 ounces sliced pepper jack cheese
1 can (2½ ounces) sliced ripe olives, drained
Hot pepper sauce (optional)

1. Remove chicken from bones and cut into strips.

2. Spoon 2 tablespoons dressing down the center of each tortilla. Top with equal amounts of lettuce, cheese, olives and chicken. Sprinkle lightly with hot pepper sauce, if desired.

3. Roll up tortillas tightly, folding in bottom.

Variation: Add chopped sun-dried tomatoes to filling.

[TIP]

Wraps and other flat breads have opened up delicious new options for hot and cold sandwich creations. Today you can choose from many kinds of flavored tortillas and taco shells. Try other ethnic breads, too. Pita bread, naan (an East Indian flat bread) and lavash (Armenian cracker bread) all make delicious detours from plain old sliced bread.

CRANBERRY-GLAZED HAM

Makes about 8 servings plus leftovers for **Delicious Ham & Cheese Puff Pie**

> 1 (5- to 6-pound) fully cooked spiral-sliced ham half
> ¾ cup cranberry sauce or cranberry chutney
> ¼ cup Dijon or spicy Dijon mustard
> 1 teaspoon ground cinnamon
> ¼ teaspoon ground allspice

1. Preheat oven to 300°F. Place ham in large roasting pan lined with heavy-duty foil. Combine cranberry sauce, mustard, cinnamon and allspice in small bowl; stir until well blended. Spread half of mixture evenly over top of ham. (Glaze will melt and spread as it cooks.)

2. Bake 1 hour. Spread remaining cranberry mixture over top of ham. Bake about 1 hour or until internal temperature of ham reaches 140°F. Transfer ham to cutting board; let stand 5 minutes before slicing.

3. Reserve and refrigerate leftover ham for Delicious Ham & Cheese Puff Pie.

DAY 2

DELICIOUS HAM & CHEESE PUFF PIE

Makes 4 to 6 servings

Ham from Cranberry-Glazed Ham
1 package (10 ounces) frozen chopped spinach, thawed and squeezed dry
1/2 cup diced red bell pepper
4 green onions, sliced
3 eggs
3/4 cup all-purpose flour
3/4 cup (3 ounces) shredded Swiss cheese
3/4 cup milk
1 tablespoon prepared mustard
1 teaspoon grated lemon peel
1 teaspoon dried dill weed
1/2 teaspoon garlic salt
1/2 teaspoon black pepper
Fresh dill sprigs and lemon slices (optional)

1. Preheat oven to 425°F. Grease round 2-quart casserole. Cut ham into bite-size pieces. You should have about 2 cups.

2. Combine ham, spinach, bell pepper and green onions in prepared casserole. Beat eggs in medium bowl. Stir in flour, cheese, milk, mustard, lemon peel, dill weed, garlic salt and black pepper; pour over ham mixture.

3. Bake 30 to 35 minutes or until puffed and browned. Cut into wedges and garnish with fresh dill and lemon slices.

INDEX

126

METRIC CONVERSION CHART

VOLUME MEASUREMENTS (dry)

$1/8$ teaspoon = 0.5 mL
$1/4$ teaspoon = 1 mL
$1/2$ teaspoon = 2 mL
$3/4$ teaspoon = 4 mL
1 teaspoon = 5 mL
1 tablespoon = 15 mL
2 tablespoons = 30 mL
$1/4$ cup = 60 mL
$1/3$ cup = 75 mL
$1/2$ cup = 125 mL
$2/3$ cup = 150 mL
$3/4$ cup = 175 mL
1 cup = 250 mL
2 cups = 1 pint = 500 mL
3 cups = 750 mL
4 cups = 1 quart = 1 L

VOLUME MEASUREMENTS (fluid)

1 fluid ounce (2 tablespoons) = 30 mL
4 fluid ounces ($1/2$ cup) = 125 mL
8 fluid ounces (1 cup) = 250 mL
12 fluid ounces ($1\frac{1}{2}$ cups) = 375 mL
16 fluid ounces (2 cups) = 500 mL

WEIGHTS (mass)

$1/2$ ounce = 15 g
1 ounce = 30 g
3 ounces = 90 g
4 ounces = 120 g
8 ounces = 225 g
10 ounces = 285 g
12 ounces = 360 g
16 ounces = 1 pound = 450 g

DIMENSIONS

$1/16$ inch = 2 mm
$1/8$ inch = 3 mm
$1/4$ inch = 6 mm
$1/2$ inch = 1.5 cm
$3/4$ inch = 2 cm
1 inch = 2.5 cm

OVEN TEMPERATURES

250°F = 120°C
275°F = 140°C
300°F = 150°C
325°F = 160°C
350°F = 180°C
375°F = 190°C
400°F = 200°C
425°F = 220°C
450°F = 230°C

BAKING PAN SIZES

Utensil	Size in Inches/Quarts	Metric Volume	Size in Centimeters
Baking or Cake Pan (square or rectangular)	$8 \times 8 \times 2$	2 L	$20 \times 20 \times 5$
	$9 \times 9 \times 2$	2.5 L	$23 \times 23 \times 5$
	$12 \times 8 \times 2$	3 L	$30 \times 20 \times 5$
	$13 \times 9 \times 2$	3.5 L	$33 \times 23 \times 5$
Loaf Pan	$8 \times 4 \times 3$	1.5 L	$20 \times 10 \times 7$
	$9 \times 5 \times 3$	2 L	$23 \times 13 \times 7$
Round Layer Cake Pan	$8 \times 1\frac{1}{2}$	1.2 L	20×4
	$9 \times 1\frac{1}{2}$	1.5 L	23×4
Pie Plate	$8 \times 1\frac{1}{4}$	750 mL	20×3
	$9 \times 1\frac{1}{4}$	1 L	23×3
Baking Dish or Casserole	1 quart	1 L	—
	$1\frac{1}{2}$ quart	1.5 L	—
	2 quart	2 L	—